BUSHLANDS AUSTRALIA

Steve Parish Publishing Pty Ltd

Australia's unique bushland

BUSHLANDS

Australians refer to the unoccupied landscapes of their country as "the bush", a term which has a multitude of meanings. Some bushland is tropical, some is temperate; some is rainforest, some is desert. All are fascinating, and full of wonderful creatures and unique plants.

For tens of thousands of years the Aboriginal people of Australia were part of the bushland, as it was part of them. Other, later comers to this wonderful continent have at times feared the bush, indeed have waged war on it, but most in time have come to respect and to love it.

The bushland has inspired the creation of images in stories and songs, in paintings and photographs. Like many others, when I am sad or thoughtful, I go to the bushland to discover again the peace that only nature can give.

In this small book, I have put together a few of my favourite bushland cameos, hoping that they will give readers as much pleasure as their originals gave me.

• Flying rainbows •

Rainbow lorikeets cling to branches, probing blossoms with their curving crimson bills and plundering sweet nectar with brush-tipped tongues. Shrieking with excitement, they launch into swift-winged flight, zipping across the sky, leaving behind echoes of their raucous calls and memories of iridescent splendour.

◆ At home in the bush ◆

A female grey kangaroo with a joey in her pouch prefers to lie up in a quiet, cool patch of bush during the heat of the day. Towards evening, she hops slowly out into the open, to graze on sweet grasses while her young one stares from its secure home, then tumbles out to play awhile.

Over: Fringed Lily

• In the treetops •

The white trunks of gum trees
hold slender leaves towards
the morning sun. On the
topmost branches, a pair of
rainbow bee-eaters prepares to
fly in pursuit of bees, wasps
and dragonflies.

The dingo, Australia's wild bushland predator.

Koalas need bush trees for their homes. Over: Tropical bushland

Native orchids, the ballerinas of the bushland.

A delicate spider orchid.

• Stay alert! •

There is danger in the bushland, and wild creatures rely on keen senses to keep them safe. A wallaby peers through the grass, alert for unfamiliar sounds or scents. A sulphur-crested cockatoo stands sentinel for its flock, watching as they feed, crest flaring in excitement as it screeches in warning.

• Spring colours •

What better colour than scarlet
to complement the muted greens
of the bush? The brilliance of
the bottlebrush signals birds
that nectar awaits within.

• Banners of welcome •

Australia's wildflowers fly
flags of welcome to insects and
birds. Deep within their hearts
they harbour nectar, a sweet
reward for the creature which
probes their depths and then
flies away, carrying pollen to
deposit on the next flower
visited.

◆ Changing guard ◆

The wombat sleeps all day and emerges
at night, to shuffle around the bushland
grazing. The kookaburra sends a
rollicking call across the sunlit trees,
intent on catching worms, insects and
snakes to eat.

• Now you see us •

Many of Australia's bush creatures remain unseen until they move. As they sleep or hide, their colours and outlines blend with trees and grass. Confident that danger is not immediate, they suddenly become visible, eyes wide, whiskers twitching and ears alert for the slightest sound.

The trees are dressing
to celebrate a new season,
leaving off their tattered bark
and donning shining new clothes.

◆ Fragile fliers ◆

The bushland harbours a myriad small lives, going about their daily business of feeding, finding a mate and producing young. Find a patch of flowers, crouch low to the ground, bring your eyes into close focus and you will discover some of nature's most exquisite creatures.

• The reclusive koala •

The koala spends most of the
day, and a good deal of the
night, sleeping. Most of the
remaining time is spent
fastidiously eating gum leaves.
There is little time left to peer
down at human visitors.

• The loud ones •

The galah (left) and yellow-tailed black-cockatoo (right) can be two of the bushland's noisiest birds. However, when they have eggs or young ones in the nests they make in hollow branches, they may be silent and unobtrusive, wary of attracting attention to their precious secrets.

Over: Eucalyptus blossom

• Beautiful banksias •

Banksias flourish on sandy, well-drained soils, where their stiff-stalked flowers provide banquets of nectar for birds, insects and small honey-eating mammals. Today, many species of these splendid flowers are cultivated, and bush-lovers can enjoy them in gardens and homes.

• Floral diversity •

Australia's bushland offers a
wide range of wildflowers,
from alpine heaths (above) to
orchids of the sand plains (left)
and the marvellous blossoms of
rainforest and desert.

◆ The all-Australian rosellas ◆

Rosellas are found in many parts of Australia. They are charming birds, fluffing their distinctive cheek-patches and flaring their broad tails as they flirt and dally with each other, confidently coming to gardens to feast on bird-table seed. The crimson rosella (left) and eastern rosella (right) are two popular and colourful members of this delightful group of parrots.

◆ Butterfly v. blossom ◆

Which is lovelier,
butterfly or blossom?
To settle the question,
we could spend fifty years
staring at blossoms,
studying butterflies,
and in the end decide
their beauty is equal –
and that the fifty years
had been well-spent.

◆ Songs of silver ◆

The Australian magpie heralds the dawn with a marvellous carolling call, the silver notes bubbling and rolling through the misty bushland. Female magpies nest alone, but once fledged their young can depend on the care of all the birds in the local family group.

• Colours of the sky •

The bushlands of southern
Australia come alive with
wildflowers in springtime.
Pinks, scarlets and yellows
spread across the ground like
gorgeous oriental carpets. Blue
blossoms do not display
themselves so lavishly. They
grow in solitary stalks of azure
beauty, or drape bushes like
swatches of silk torn from the
cloudless sky above.

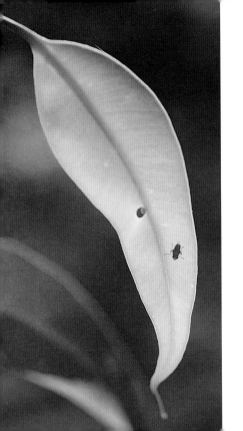

• Floral symbols •

A simple flower can be a strong reminder of home for the wandering Australian. Gum leaves symbolise Australia and, on the other side of the world, a whiff of eucalyptus can inspire the traveller to make the tearful purchase of a ticket home. The mountain devil symbolises the magnificent sandstone landscapes of the Blue Mountains of New South Wales.

A majestic symbol of Australia, a eucalypt or gum tree.

Another symbol of Australia, the koala. Over: Eucalyptus blossom

• Misty mornings •

The bushland is not always drenched in sunshine. Mist and rain add subtle charm to a landscape, with leaves dew-pearled and the songs of birds echoing from valleys shrouded in soft, silver mystery.

Young emu

Young red-necked wallaby

• Nature's lessons •

Tall wet forests,
parched dry deserts,
sand plains, where flowers
carpet the ground,
ancient rocks
and wide, flooded plains –
the bushland
is full of living things,
all waiting to share their secrets
with you, and with me,
if we are willing
to listen, watch and learn.

Steve Parish has recorded Australia, its wildlife and its people with his camera for many years. Steve's aim is to show people the marvels that exist in this long-isolated continent, with its unique cities, landscapes, plants and animals. His passion for Australia, and his awareness that urgent human action is needed to preserve its wildlife and places of beauty lends intensity to his superb photographs and evocative writing. Steve and his wife and partner Jan founded Steve Parish Publishing Pty Ltd to share with the world their vision of Australia.

Steve Parish
PUBLISHING

© Copyright photography and text Steve Parish Publishing Pty Ltd 1997
First published in Australia by Steve Parish Publishing Pty Ltd
PO Box 2160 Fortitude Valley BC Queensland 4006 Australia

Text: Pat Slater

PRINTED IN AUSTRALIA

ISBN 1 875932 73 9